Wendy
and the
WHINE

Library of Congress Cataloging-in-Publication Data

Greene, Carol.
    Wendy and the whine.

    Summary: Wendy learns through prayer and her grandmother's guidance that the habit of whining can be overcome with the help of the Lord.
    [1. Conduct of life—Fiction. 2. Christian life—Fiction] I. Title.
PZ7.G82845Wen 1987   [E]   86-18813
ISBN 0-570-04157-0

1 2 3 4 5 6 7 8 9 10   DP   96 95 94 93 92 91 90 89 88 87

Wendy
and the
WHINE

by Carol Greene
illustrated by Will Hardin

CONCORDIA®
Publishing House
St. Louis

Wendy Winston did not *want* to whine. But when you're the middle kid in the family and you *need* something . . . well . . . sometimes whining is the only way to be heard. At least that's how it seemed to Wendy.

But one of the problems with whining is that after a while you don't even hear yourself doing it. Your family and friends hear you, though. And they don't like it very much.

Sometimes friends get so tired of whiners that they don't even want to be with them. After all, who wants to hear someone who sounds like a police siren all the time? That's how Wendy's friends felt.

But Wendy didn't *really* worry about her whining till the day of Baby's birthday party.

It was just a small family party after supper. Baby was only one year old. But everyone gave her a present, and she chewed up the wrapping paper and made happy noises.

Then Mom brought in the cake. It was the most beautiful birthday cake Wendy had ever seen, with blue frosting and pink sugar roses—*two* pink sugar roses.

"Come on, Baby. Blow out the candle," urged everyone. Then everyone blew out the candle for her and told Baby how clever she was.

"And here's the first piece for the birthday girl," said Mom. She put a piece of cake—with a pink sugar rose—on Baby's plate.

"Hey, Mom, can I have the other rose?" asked Wendy's big brother Joe in his big, loud voice.

"Why, I suppose . . . " began Mom. But Wendy didn't let her finish.

"Aw, Mom, I want the rose," she whined. "Come on, Mom. Let me have it. I *neeeeed* it!"

HEY!

And then something remarkable happened. That Whine leaped right out of Wendy's mouth and rushed around the room like a little imp of a breeze with a mind all its own.

Eeeee! It tickled Mom's ear.

"Please stop that, Wendy," said Mom.

Eeeee! It ruffled Dad's hair.

"Cut it out, Wendy!" said Dad.

Eeeee! It knocked Joe's glasses crooked.

"Hey!" yelled Joe.

At last the Whine got back to Wendy. Quick as could be, she grabbed it and popped it back into her mouth. Then she swallowed . . . hard.

"Wendy, dear," said her mom, "you really must do something about that whining. It is becoming most unpleasant."

"But, Mom," whined Wendy. "This time it wasn't my fauuuult!"

That was all it took. Out leaped the Whine again. Only this time it was bigger and stronger—like a frisky gust of wind with a naughty gleam in its eye.

Awwww! It flapped the curtains at the window.

Awwww! It tangled the tablecloth.

Awwww! It blew Baby's new stuffed giraffe right into the middle of the birthday cake.

"Waaaah!" yelled Baby.

Once again Wendy grabbed the Whine and stuffed it into her mouth. But she was too late. Her whole family was staring at her.

"You better get out of here, Wendy," said Joe. "You're ruining everything."

Wendy went. She didn't say a word. She couldn't. Her mouth was too full of Whine.

Wendy flopped down on her bed. Once again she swallowed hard. Then, very carefully, she opened her mouth. No Whine.

"Whew!" said Wendy. She picked up her teddy bear.

"What happened, Sam?" she whispered. "*I didn't* make those awful noises. They just . . . just came out of me. But nobody's going to believe that. They'll blame *me.* What am I going to do, Sam?"

Sam didn't answer her. He just twinkled his bright black eyes and looked comforting. That was all he ever did.

But suddenly Wendy had an idea.

"You know what, Sam?" she whispered. "It's harder to whine when you whisper. Not *impossible*, but harder. Maybe I'll just whisper to everyone from now on."

She began the next morning at breakfast.

"May I have a banana on my cereal?" she whispered.

"Huh?" said Joe in his loud voice.

"Wendy, does your throat hurt?" asked her mom. She felt Wendy's forehead to see if she had a fever.

"Umpf," said her dad, who wasn't listening anyway.

"I do not have a sore throat," whispered Wendy. "I am just not whining."

"You're a weird little kid," said Joe.

"Umpf," said her dad, who wasn't listening anyway.

"Well, good for you, dear," said her mom. But she forgot to give Wendy a banana for her cereal.

Next, Wendy tried whispering to her friends on the school bus.

"Hi, Donna. Hi, Joshua. Hi, Jimmy," she hissed.

"What's the matter, Wendy? Cat got your tongue?" they all asked. Then they meowed at her all the way to school.

"Very funny," whispered Wendy.

But the real trouble started when she tried to whisper in school.

"Wendy Winston, can you tell us the capital of Norway?" asked Miss Jones.

"Yes, ma'am," whispered Wendy. "It's Oslo."

"You'll have to speak up, Wendy," said Miss Jones.

Wendy tried to whisper louder. "I said, it's Oslo."

"I'm sorry, Wendy," said Miss Jones in a voice that didn't sound sorry at all. "You will have to speak up or else be marked incorrect."

That made Wendy so nervous that, without think-ing, she spoke up.

"I said Oslohhhh!" she whined.

It was out.

OSLO-0-0-0

Ohhhh! It raced around the room like a whirlwind, scattering books, papers, and little Jimmy Schmid-lapp as it went. And its face looked downright mean.

Ohhhh! It spun Miss Jones in circles and sucked all the pins out of her hair.

Wendy tried to catch it the way she had before . . . but she couldn't. It was too big now and too fast.

Ohhhh! It swooped out an open window and disappeared.

"What was *that?*" asked little Jimmy Schmidlapp from under a pile of spelling tests.

"I don't know," said Donna Dingby.

"Let's ask Miss Jones," said Joshua Gugliano.

"Where *is* Miss Jones?" asked little Jimmy Schmidlapp.

They found her scrunched up under her desk with her hands over her ears.

"Oh! Children!" she said and quickly crawled out. "My goodness, wasn't that a strange meteorological phenomenon we just observed?"

"Is *that* what it was?" asked Donna Dingby.

"Well, of course," said Miss Jones. "Now, back to your seats, children. Let's see, where were we? Oh, yes. Joshua Gugliano, can you tell us the capital of Sweden?"

Wendy didn't say anything. But she knew the whirlwind hadn't been any meteorological phenomenon. It had been her Whine.

Wendy pressed her lips together as tightly as she could. She would not talk to anyone . . . not ever again for as long as she lived. It was the only way to keep the world safe from that Whine. Fortunately, Miss Jones didn't call on her anymore.

But Wendy found it a lot harder to stay quiet when she got home.

"Hello, darling," said her mom. "How was school?" She kissed Wendy on the ear.

"Mmf," said Wendy through her tightly pressed lips.

"As bad as all that?" said her mom. "Poor dear. Well, never mind. I want you to go upstairs, wash your face and hands, and comb your hair. Dad's coming home early, and we're all driving out to Grandma's for supper."

Wendy's heart sank. Grandma's house was the last place she wanted to go. Not that she didn't like it. She loved it. And that was the problem. Grandma was such a . . . well . . . special person that Wendy knew she could never be quiet around her. Sooner or later, she'd say something—and *pow!* Out would pop that Whine.

Glumly she washed her face and hands and combed her hair. Then, suddenly, Wendy had an idea. She opened the medicine cabinet and took out a plastic dispenser. Then, very carefully, she tied a long piece of gauze over her mouth. There! Now she *couldn't* talk.

When she got back downstairs, the rest of her family was already waiting for her at the front door.

"Wendy!" cried her mom. "What happened to your mouth?"

Wendy ran into the kitchen. She got a piece of paper and a crayon. She printed two words on the paper. Then she ran back and showed them to her family.

"Sore lips," the words said.

It was true, too. Her lips really did feel sore after pressing them together all that time.

"What on earth?" said her dad.

"Boy, are you *weird,*" said Joe.

But her mom just smiled and patted Wendy on the head. "Never mind," she said. "It's probably just a phase. She'll outgrow it."

Wendy tried to smile back at her. But it is very difficult to smile with gauze over your mouth.

When they got to Grandma's, everyone sat in the living room and talked for a while. Everyone except Wendy. She sat there holding up her piece of paper. Grandma didn't seem at all surprised. But, then, Grandma was good at not seeming surprised. She just dumped her big orange cat in Wendy's lap and went on talking with everyone else.

Before long it was time to eat. And that was when Wendy remembered something very important and very horrible. You cannot eat with gauze over your mouth.

There she sat, at the table, staring at the big bowl of chicken and dumplings—her favorite food.

"Rowr!" said her stomach. "Rowr!"

"Don't be so dumb, Wendy," said Joe. "Take off the gauze so you can eat."

"Mmf," said Wendy. But she didn't touch the gauze. She didn't dare.

"Okay," said Joe. "I'll take it off for you."

He got up and pulled off the strip of gauze. He also pulled Wendy's hair.

"OWWWW!" whined Wendy.

OWWWW! Suddenly the whole room seemed sucked into a tornado.

OWWWW! Chicken and dumplings flew in all directions. Baby snatched a drumstick as it whirled past and began to chew on it. An extremely large dumpling smacked Dad right in the face.

OWWWW! The Whine began to juggle the dishes, then the table and chairs.

"Down!" shouted Dad, grabbing Baby. "Everyone get down and cover your head!"

And everyone did . . . except Grandma. She calmly marched over to a window, opened it, and said in a firm voice, "*You* may be excused."

Owwww? Just like that, the Whine softened to a murmur. Carefully it put the furniture, dishes and food back where they belonged. Then, meekly, it trickled out the window.

"And that," said Grandma, slamming down the window, "is that."

"But *what* was it?" asked Joe in his loud voice. "I mean, wow! I mean, I heard about this meteorological phenomenon at school today. It was in your room, wasn't it, Wendy? I mean, do you think that maybe . . . ?"

"Please lower your voice, Joe," interrupted Grandma. "And the rest of you will please oblige me by going on with your meal. Wendy and I are going into the living room to have a talk."

"Yes, Grandma," said everyone. There were times when you simply didn't argue with Grandma.

Wendy followed her into the living room and curled up in a sad little ball in the corner of the couch. Grandma sat down in her rocking chair, and the big orange cat jumped up into her lap.

"Now," said Grandma, "tell me about it."

So Wendy told her—about Baby's birthday party and the giraffe in the cake. About the day at school and poor little Jimmy Schmidlapp and the meteorological phenomenon that wasn't a meteorological phenomenon at all.

"It's a Whine," concluded Wendy, "a horrible monster Whine that comes out of *me*. And I don't know what to do about it."

"I see," said Grandma. "And I think that this is something you need to pray to the Lord about, Wendy. Would you prefer to do that alone or here with me?"

"Oh, here—please," said Wendy. Somehow she felt safer with Grandma around. Both of them folded their hands and bowed their heads.

"Dear Lord," prayed Wendy, "I have this terrific problem. It's a Whine. You've probably heard it Yourself by now. I want to get rid of it, Lord. But I don't know how. Please help me. Amen."

She looked at Grandma. "Well?" she asked. "What next?"

"Hush, child," said Grandma. "When you're through praying, you need to listen, too. Be quiet now and listen."

So Wendy listened. But all she could hear was the creak-creak of Grandma's rocking chair and the purrs of the big orange cat.

"I have it!" said Grandma so suddenly that the cat jumped off her lap and hid under the couch. "I have an idea!"

"You do?" said Wendy. "Did the Lord give it to you?"

"All good things come from the Lord," replied Grandma. "James said so in the Bible. And this is definitely a good idea. A Whine, you see, is a habit. A bad habit. And habits are usually things we do without thinking. As soon as we start thinking about them, we're on our way to breaking them."

Wendy nodded. "That makes sense."

"So," continued Grandma, "from now on, you must think before you speak. Before you say anything at all, you must repeat to yourself silently, 'A Whine is a loathsome and troublesome thing.' By the time you have said that, you will have remembered not to whine."

"A Whine is a loathsome and troublesome thing," repeated Wendy. She began to giggle. "I don't think I can say that—not even silently—without laughing."

"All the better," said Grandma. "It is very difficult to whine when you are laughing."

"Do you suppose I'll have to go on saying it for the rest of my life?" asked Wendy.

"Of course not," said Grandma. "Just until you've broken the habit. Now, let's thank the Lord for His help. Then we'll go back in and have our supper."

They both bowed their heads and folded their hands again.

"Thank You, Lord," said Wendy. "Thank You for the good idea. Thank You for Grandma. Thank You for *all* good things. Amen."

It was a delicious supper, the best supper Wendy had ever eaten. She stuffed herself until she thought she would pop. Then she decided to tell Grandma how good it had been.

Very carefully she repeated to herself, "A Whine is a loathsome and troublesome thing." Then she opened her mouth. Out came a giggle.

"What's so funny?" asked Joe.

"A Whine is a loathsome and troublesome thing," said Wendy. "Oh, hee hee hee!"

"Huh?" said Joe in his loudest voice. "What's *loathsome?*"

"I don't know," said Wendy. "Oh, ho ho!"

"Loathsome," said Grandma, "means . . . er . . . very icky. And I'll thank you to lower your voice, Joe."

"Loathsome," said Joe quietly. *"Loathsome!"* He dissolved into giggles too.

Soon Mom was saying it, then Dad, then Grandma. Before long, everyone was laughing themselves silly.

Meanwhile, outside, a weak-looking Whine crept up to the window and peered in. But when it saw all those laughing people it jumped back in horror. Then, with a great shudder, it turned away and disappeared into the night forever.

Every good gift . . . is from above.
James 1:17